The Truth (& Myths) about Sea Monsters

by L. A. Peacock

illustrated by Nick Wigsby

Scholastic Inc.

For Cousin Ernie and Naomi, with love—L.A.F.

Photos ©: 11, 12: Courtesy of the Calvert Marine Museum, Solomons, Maryland; 18: Keystone/Getty Images; 21: North Wind Picture Archives/AP Images; 25: Snikeltrut/Thinkstock; 27: Fortean/TopFoto/The Image Works; 29 top: Mint Images - Frans Lanting/Getty Images; 29 bottom: Reinhard Dirscherl/Getty Images; 30: Dorling Kindersley/Thinkstock; 31: Geoff Kidd/Science Source; 32: Jeremy Stafford-Deitsch/Science Source; 35: Jeff Rotman/Science Source; 37: Krzysztof Odziomek/Thinkstock; 39, 60: Fred Bavendam/Minden Pictures; 40: Everett Collection; 41: Sean Rowland/Covered Images/Zumapress via Newscom; 43: Tabgac/Dreamstime; 45: Photos 12/Alamy Images; 46: Crisod/Dreamstime; 49: Christopher Meder/Thinkstock; 50: Evgeniya Lazareva/Thinkstock; 54: Richard Fitzer/Shutterstock, Inc.; 55: Konrad Mostert/Thinkstock; 57: Ingram Publishing/Thinkstock; 58: AP Images; 62: Danita Delimont/Alamy Images; 64: Teguh Tirtaputra/Shutterstock, Inc.; 69: ANT Photo Library/Science Source; 70: Jany Sauvanet/Science Source; 72: Flirt/Superstock; 74: Gregory G. Dimijian/Science Source; 76: Bkamprath/Thinkstock; 77: Paul Cowell/Shutterstock, Inc.; 79: Suthep Kritsanavarin/AP Images; 80: imageBroker/Alamy Images; 82: Doc White/naturepl.com/NaturePL; 83: Jxpfeer/Dreamstime; 84: William R. Curtsinger/National Geographic Creative; 85: Kerryn Parkinson/Norfanz/Caters News/Zuma Press; 87: Kathy Willens/AP Images; 89: Connie Bransilver/Science Source.

ISBN 978-0-545-70566-0

12 11 10 9 8 7 6 5 4   21/0

Printed in the U.S.A.   40

First edition, January 2015

Contents

Chapter 1
Oceans of the World

What did the earth look like 250 million years ago?

There was one giant landmass called **Pangaea** (pan-JEE-uh), with the ocean surrounding it. This was the beginning of the Mesozoic, or the Age of Reptiles. Dinosaurs ruled the earth, and scary marine animals filled the seas.

What happened over time?

The landmass pulled apart, forming seven continents. Even today, the earth continues to change. Powerful storms, earthquakes, and **tsunamis** reshape coastlines. Volcanoes, deep on the ocean floor, create new islands. The earth may look very different in another 100 million years.

PANGAEA

How much water is in the five oceans?

About 97.2 percent of all water on earth is in the oceans. Only 2.8 percent of the rest is freshwater that is found in lakes, ponds, and rivers.

The main island of Hawaii is the world's tallest mountain.

TRUTH! It's a volcanic island, measuring 33,476 feet from its base on the ocean floor to its highest peak on land. Mount Everest, the world's highest peak, is 29,029 feet above sea level.

Where is the deepest part of the ocean?

In the **abyss**, at the bottom of the Mariana Trench, about seven miles down in the center of the Pacific Ocean. The seabed is not always flat. There are deep canyons, such as the Mariana Trench, and volcanic mountains in the abyss.

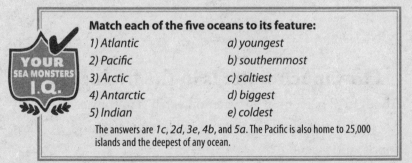

YOUR SEA MONSTERS I.Q.

Match each of the five oceans to its feature:

1) Atlantic	a) youngest
2) Pacific	b) southernmost
3) Arctic	c) saltiest
4) Antarctic	d) biggest
5) Indian	e) coldest

The answers are *1c, 2d, 3e, 4b,* and *5a*. The Pacific is also home to 25,000 islands and the deepest of any ocean.

What is the smallest and most plentiful organism in the ocean?

Plankton makes up 90 percent of ocean life. It consists of tiny plants and animals. There are millions of organisms in one cup of ocean water.

Why is plankton so important?

It is at the bottom of the ocean **food chain**. Blue whales are near the top. These giants eat **krill**, a kind of zooplankton, or very small shrimp that feed on other plankton. One blue whale eats up to 8,000 pounds of krill every day.

What are the simplest ocean animals?

The **invertebrates**, such as sponges and coral. They have no backbone. Starfish, sand dollars, snails, and even the giant squid are all invertebrates.

When is an animal considered a fish?

If it has a backbone and **gills**. Most fish have bony skeletons. Some fish, such as sharks, have skeletons made of **cartilage**. It's hard and rubbery—the same material found in human ears and noses.

THERE ARE MORE THAN 24,000 SPECIES OF FISH.

THE BIGGEST FISH IS THE WHALE SHARK.

IT CAN GROW TO 60 FEET.

TRUTH or MYTH?

Fish breathe air like humans do.

MYTH! They don't breathe air. Fish live underwater all the time. They take their oxygen from the water through special filters called gills. The oxygen then passes into the fish's blood and body.

GILLS

Chapter 2
Prehistoric Seas

How do we know so much about prehistoric times?

From **fossils**. These are the remains of plant and creatures that lived millions of years ago. Many fossils are made from animal bones or shells that have been preserved in rocks.

Where were most fossils formed?

Underwater, at the bottom of lakes, rivers, or seas. Dead **prehistoric** creatures were buried in layers of mud and sand, which slowly hardened. The creature's skeleton was turned into a fossil. Over millions of years, these fossils were pushed up out of the water. Today, we find fossils on land, in layers of **sedimentary** rocks.

What about the footprints of prehistoric animals?

These are called trace fossils. The eggs and droppings that are left behind by prehistoric animals are trace fossils, too.

When did fish first appear in the fossil record?

Fish were the first animals to have backbones. These **vertebrates** appeared about 510 million years ago.

TRUTH or MYTH?

The first fish had jaws for opening and closing their mouths.

MYTH! The earliest fish lived on the seabed. They sucked up small pieces of food along the sea floor.

When did fish with jaws appear?

About 420 million years ago. Most were fierce hunters.

THE FIRST SHARKS APPEARED ABOUT THIS TIME, TOO.

How big were these early bony fish?

Some were gigantic. The *Dunkleosteus* reached 30 feet in length.

Did *Dunkleosteus* have sharp teeth?

Yes, but they weren't real teeth. They had two sharp bony blades along the jawbone that worked like a beak. The fish used these blades to bite down on **prey**.

What came first—dinosaurs or sharks?

Sharks were here first, about 200 million years before dinosaurs.

How do we know about prehistoric sharks?

They left almost no fossils, because shark skeletons are made of cartilage, not bone. But plenty of teeth have been found. These teeth are more than twice as big as the teeth of today's great white shark.

How big are the teeth of prehistoric sharks?

Up to six inches! These belong to huge sharks called *Megalodon*. The name means "giant tooth" in ancient Greek.

What did these sharks look like?

The **fossil record** suggests that *Megalodon* reached 59 feet in length. It looked a lot like today's great white shark.

How big were its jaws?

The giant jaws of *Megalodon* were about seven feet high and six feet across. The jaws of the largest great white are only about two feet wide.

Without a complete skeleton, how do we know this?

Bashford Dean was the first to reconstruct a *Megalodon* jaw in 1909. He used fossil teeth from different locations. From his jaw reconstruction, Dean estimated the length of the *Megalodon* to be 98 feet. With today's methods, scientists now believe it to be about 70 percent of that size.

Why did these giant sharks disappear?

They ran out of food. The fossil record suggests that during the Ice Age the oceans cooled when **glaciers** were formed. The *Megalodon* became **extinct** as it lost its warm-water **habitats**. It no longer had plentiful food for itself and its young.

When did reptiles start entering the seas?

About 315 million years ago. These sea reptiles had bodies that were adapted for living underwater. They looked like lizards and snakes. Some had long, thin bodies. Flippers took the place of legs. Some had webbed feet for easy swimming. Most had powerful jaws and big sharp teeth for catching fish. They were fierce-looking creatures.

What was one of the biggest of these sea reptiles?

At 80 feet long, the *Liopleurodon* was the biggest meat eater ever. It was twenty times heavier than a *T. rex*.

What did *Liopleurodon* look like?

It had a long body. There were two flippers on each side. Its head was more than ten feet long, with powerful, crocodile-like jaws.

THEY HAD NOSES ON BIG HEADS.

THEY COULD SMELL THEIR PREY UNDERWATER!

Was the *Liopleurodon* a good swimmer?

Yes. Its limbs were strong and acted like paddles, so it could propel through the water at a good speed.

Were there other giant sea reptiles?

Prehistoric seas were filled with many kinds of sea monsters. *Elasmosaurus* was another giant at 46 feet long and two tons in weight. It had an extremely long neck, about half its body length.

WRONG END, EDWARD!

What mistake was made when *Elasmosaurus* fossils were found more than one hundred years ago?

The scientist Edward Drinker Cope put the fossils together incorrectly. He placed the head on the short end. This was the *wrong* end—the creature's tail! It was an easy mistake to make. Cope was an expert on lizards, which have a short neck and a long tail.

Chapter 3
Tales of Sea Monsters

Did people long ago know about sea monsters?

Carvings on rocks 4,000 years ago showed men hunting big sea animals. From ancient times, peoples' early writings of sea voyages are filled with stories of sea creatures and terrible beasts.

What did these creatures look like?

Horrible creatures appear on ocean maps of the 16th century. One sea monster was the water horse, with its long body and neck showing above the water. This "aquatic dinosaur" was a favorite of sailors' stories in many **folk traditions**.

What's the most famous water horse story?

As far back as the year AD 565, there have been reports of a giant reptile-like animal in Scotland's Loch Ness.

LOCH IS THE SCOTTISH WORD FOR LAKE.

When did the "Nessie" legend begin?

Reports of monsters in the Scottish lochs began in the Middle Ages, with claims of people seeing "dragons" in the River Ness. In modern times, newspapers ran stories of "Nessie" sightings. These animals were said to have large bodies and long thin necks. They had fins, extended tails, and were up to 30 feet long.

Why is Loch Ness a good place to look for sea monsters?

The lake is big and old. It's about 23 miles long and 800 feet deep. Loch Ness was formed 10,000 years ago during the Ice Age. When the glaciers melted, animals from the Atlantic Ocean could have washed into the lake—including "large beasts" as the legend suggests.

We have photos of the Loch Ness monster.

TRUTH! But we're not sure they're real. A photo taken in April 1934 by R.K. Wilson claimed to show a "long-necked" Nessie. But another photo taken at the same time suggested Wilson actually photographed a seal or otter.

What was discovered about the photo in 1994?

That photograph got a lot of publicity, but it turned out to be a **hoax** staged by Marmaduke Wetherell, who persuaded R. K. Wilson to sell it to a newspaper as his own. This fake image was actually a plastic toy made to look like Nessie.

Does the U.S. have its own Nessie?

The best known is "Champs." This creature is said to live in Lake Champlain, located between New York, Vermont, and Canada. In 1609, the explorer Samuel de Champlain claimed to have seen a large snakelike creature with the head of a horse swimming in the lake.

Are there any other American sea-monster tales?

For years, drivers crossing the floating bridge of Lake Washington in Washington State reported seeing a big, dark object in the lake. In 1987, the mystery creature washed ashore. It turned out to be a giant sturgeon. This fish measured 11 feet long and weighed 900 pounds. These big fish have been around for 135 million years. Scientists believe they are behind the reports of Champs and Nessie.

Chapter 4
Early Ocean Adventurers

In the Bible story, what happened when Jonah disobeyed God?

Jonah tried to escape on a sailing ship. But God sent strong winds and waves, so Jonah's ship sank. Jonah was swallowed by a giant fish. After three days and nights in the fish's belly, Jonah was forgiven and the fish coughed him up alive.

What American Founding Father was interested in ocean currents?

Benjamin Franklin. He proved that American ships traveled faster when they used ocean **currents** to sail to Europe. He was the first to put together reports from sea captains and draw a map of the Gulf Stream, an important current in the Atlantic Ocean.

Where did 19th century writers of sea stories get their ideas?

Mostly from whalers who had their own fish stories. The most famous one of all was *Moby Dick* by Herman Melville. It was based on stories from seamen and Melville's year at sea as a Pacific whaler in 1841.

TRUTH or MYTH?

There was a real whale called Moby Dick.

TRUTH! Melville's story was based on the true accounts of a huge sperm whale named Mocha Dick. From 1810, this whale attacked whaleboats. It was finally killed in 1859. Nineteen harpoons were stuck in its body.

What inspired Jules Verne to write his 1870 book, *20,000 Leagues under the Sea*?

A trip to the aquarium. On an Atlantic crossing, Verne also gathered stories from crew members. They had laid the Atlantic telegraph cable the year before. His famous novel told about a giant squid attacking a ship.

When did the scientific study of the oceans get its start?

Oceanography began with the British Royal Navy *Challenger* expedition of 1872–76. It was led by the scientist Charles Wyville Thomson and the mapmaker Captain George Strong Nares.

How did the crew measure ocean depth?

With rope. They lowered a line with weights attached until it reached the ocean floor.

Did the *Challenger* collect samples from the seabed?

Yes. The sinker line carried a small container that was dragged along the bottom. The crew also swept metal nets along the ocean floor to collect samples.

What did they find about 14,000 feet down on the seabed in 1875?

A *Megalodon* tooth. It was thought to be about 11,000 years old, which is not that old in geological time. Some scientists believe that there are *Megalodons* alive today. They just haven't found one yet.

Chapter 5
Living Sea Fossils

What's one of the oldest kinds of fish living today?

The lampreys. They have rounded, sucking mouths but no jaws.

BACK OFF, BOTTOM-FEEDERS!!

How long have lampreys been in the oceans?

Lamprey fossils date back to 360 million years ago.

Are lampreys good to eat?

English royalty thought so. During the Middle Ages, King Henry I is said to have died from eating too many lampreys. In 1953, Queen Elizabeth II's coronation pie was made from lampreys.

YUMMY!

Why are horseshoe crabs called "living dinosaurs"?

They've remained mostly the same for more than 300 million years.

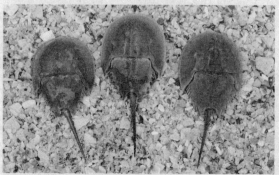

Where do horseshoe crabs get their name?

From the shape of their shell. These marine invertebrates can grow to about 24 inches as an adult. Their natural diet is shellfish and worms.

TRUTH or MYTH?

The horseshoe crab's tail holds a stinger filled with **venom**.

MYTH! The tail isn't poisonous. The animal uses its tail to turn itself over if it lands on its back.

HELP!!

USE YOUR TAIL!

Where can you find the horseshoe crab's mouth?

In the center of its body, where its five pairs of legs meet. The top of the legs serve as jaws to grind up food.

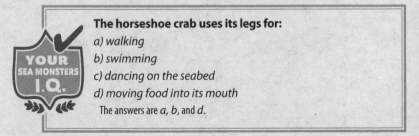

YOUR SEA MONSTERS I.Q.

The horseshoe crab uses its legs for:

a) walking
b) swimming
c) dancing on the seabed
d) moving food into its mouth

The answers are *a*, *b*, and *d*.

Did early sailors really see terrifying sea serpents?

They probably saw large eels that looked like sea serpents. The biggest and oldest is the oarfish, which can grow up to 36 feet long.

What does an oarfish look like?

Like a sea serpent. Its short, blunt head is bluish in color. The fins that stick out from the side of its head are bright red. The oarfish is rarely seen alive or caught.

TRUTH or MYTH?

Oarfish have an unusual way of swimming.

TRUTH! They float most of the time. They keep their heads up vertically and extend their long bodies near the water's surface.

Can oarfish predict earthquakes?

A Japanese myth says that when an oarfish washes up on a beach, an earthquake is coming. About 20 oarfish beached themselves in Japan before the 2011 earthquake and tsunami!

What is the Kraken?

A famous mythical sea beast known in folklore since the Middle Ages. Scientists today believe it was a giant octopus or giant squid.

IT'S THAT *KRAKEN* AGAIN!

TRUTH or MYTH?

Giant squids attack submarines and sailing ships.

MYTH! There is no evidence of these attacks, although giant squids are able to grab large objects. They have eight thick arms and two longer tentacles, which they use to bring prey into their beak-shaped mouth.

How big can giant squids get?

Giant squids can reach lengths of 40 feet and weigh 1,000 pounds or more. They live in very deep water. Few have been seen alive. The one that washed up on the coast north of Boston in the 1980s measured 32.8 feet long. The giant squid is the largest invertebrate in the world.

How do they swim?

The giant squid uses fins along its head to propel forward. It also jets water to pick up speed quickly. Special ink sacs can release ink to defend against a **predator**, such as the giant sperm whale.

What color are the giant squid's eyes?

Blue, and they're big! The eye of the giant squid can measure up to 10 inches in diameter.

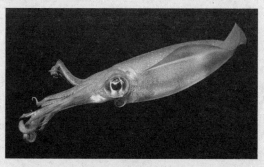

Chapter 6
Sharks

How old are sharks?

They've been swimming in the world's oceans for 400 million years—about 200 million years before the dinosaurs.

TRUTH or MYTH?

Sharks have gills like fish, but they don't swim like other fish.

TRUTH! A fish swims like a snake wiggles. With S-shaped motions, the fish propels its body and tail forward. Many sharks cruise near the water's surface. They beat their tails from side to side and use their fins to move forward. The dorsal fin on top keeps the shark from rolling onto its side.

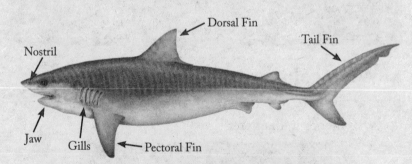

Dorsal Fin

Tail Fin

Nostril

Jaw

Gills

Pectoral Fin

Why can the shark move so easily?

It's **flexible** because its skeleton is made of cartilage, not bone like other fish.

Is losing teeth a problem for sharks?

No. Another tooth rotates up as a replacement when one is lost. A shark's jaw typically has two to three working rows of teeth with 20 to 30 teeth in each row—and they often fall out. When a tooth in the front row is lost, a replacement tooth moves up.

How many teeth can some sharks produce?

More than 30,000 teeth in a lifetime. It takes eight to ten days to grow a new tooth. Different sharks have different teeth, depending on what they eat. Some have several types of teeth.

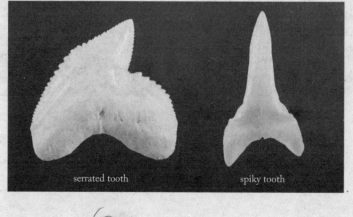

serrated tooth   spiky tooth

SERRATED TEETH RIP APART SEALS AND OTHER BIG PREY.

SPIKY TEETH HELP TO CATCH PREY, SUCH AS FISH.

Why is the great white shark a "perfect" killing machine?

It's fast and strong. The great white can attack its prey at 30 mph. A second before striking, the shark's snout rises. The shark leads with its upper jaws. The force of the bite is so great that the shark can carry up to 220 pounds of prey in its mouth as it leaps up out of the water.

How strong are shark teeth?

A great white's tooth tip pushes down at a pressure of more than 40,000 pounds per square inch. A human tooth can press only 150 pounds!

GREAT WHITES CAN ATTACK BY SURPRISE FROM BELOW.

THEY HUNT PREY AS LARGE AS ELEPHANT SEALS AND BIG SQUIDS.

JAWS

How do sharks find their fish dinner before they see it?

They detect the fish's heartbeat with ESP, or "electric sensory preceptors." These are the ampullae of Lorenzini, a network of tiny tubes in the shark's snout. They let the shark know that prey is close by.

SHARKS CAN DETECT A SWIMMER'S HEARTBEAT FROM A MILE AWAY!

How can they pick up vibrations in the water?

Sharks have a **lateral line** of pores running along the sides of their bodies from head to tail. Tiny hairs in these pores sense changes in water pressure caused by movements of other fish or predators in the area.

How well do sharks smell?

Their sense of smell is thousands of times better than ours. Some sharks can smell one drop of blood in 25 million drops of ocean water. By comparison, a rat can smell food only 20 feet away.

TRUTH or MYTH?

Sharks will eat anything.

MYTH! They're picky eaters. All sharks are **carnivores**. Sharks sometimes take a sample bite. If they don't like the taste, they spit it out and swim away.

How far do great white sharks travel?

Some can make the 6,897-mile trip from South Africa to Australia in just ninety-nine days.

Why is the great white shark able to swim so far and so fast?

It has an efficient **metabolism** and blood-circulatory system. It swims at high speeds even in cold water because it can maintain a body temperature well above that of the surrounding water.

How are sharks able to navigate over great distances?

They have a built-in "GPS" that acts like a compass. Instead of having a magnetic needle pointing north, the shark can sense changes in their own electronic field in relation to the earth's magnetic field.

Are scientists able to study sharks?

Yes. They often observe the big ones close up in underwater cages. Electronic tags are used to track shark **migration** and breeding patterns.

How big is the great white?

The biggest ever caught was 20 feet 8 inches long. It weighed 5,085 pounds.

TRUTH or MYTH?

All sharks are dangerous to humans.

MYTH! Many are not. The basking shark grows to 50 feet. The whale shark, the world's largest fish, grows to 60 feet and can weigh 13 tons. Unlike the great white, these species are no threat to people.

Do whale sharks have big mouths?

Yes, about 4.6 feet wide. That's almost as wide as the front of a car.

How much do they eat in one day?

About 3,000 pounds of food.

TRUTH or MYTH?

All whale sharks look alike.

MYTH! Each has a unique pattern of spots, like human fingerprints.

How many kinds of sharks are there?

About 375 different species. The smallest is the dwarf lantern shark at four inches. The deadliest is the great white. The longest-living is the whale shark. It can live up to 150 years, while most sharks live up to 20 or 30 years.

Who's the fastest?
a) a bottlenose dolphin
b) a killer whale
c) a mako shark

The answer is *c*. Makos, at 31 mph, are faster than dolphins at 22 mph. But killer whales, at 30 mph, are almost as fast.

What sharks have the strangest-shaped heads?

The hammerheads, with their broad, flat, hammer-shaped heads. There are nine species. The great hammerheads can reach 19.5 feet in length.

Why do hammerheads swing their heads side to side as they swim?

To see. Their eyes are located at the tops of their hammers. Also, the ampullae of Lorenzini are located here. They are used to sense the electric current given off by their prey.

What's their favorite food?

Stingrays. And they don't mind getting stung. One hammerhead was found with 100 stingers sticking into its mouth and stomach.

Are there a lot of movies about man-eating sharks?

Yes, and they get big audiences. The 1975 movie *Jaws* featured a great white feeding on summer swimmers.

Do sharks like to eat people?

The big ones, like the great white, prefer fatty seals. Attacks on humans are rare. There are fewer than 100 reported shark attacks on people and only about ten deaths worldwide each year.

Fisherman Humphrey Simmons caught a tiger shark. What did he find when he slit it open?

The remains of a sailor. The shark had burped up the missing sailor's foot, but most of him was still inside.

YOUR SEA MONSTERS I.Q.

You are more likely to die of a shark attack than:
a) to die from a bee sting
b) to be struck by lightning
c) to be killed by a tornado
d) to become a professional football player
None of the above. Death by shark is the least likely to happen.

Why do surfers on small body boards attract sharks?

A person with arms and legs dangling from a boogie board looks from below like a shark's favorite food—a seal or sea lion!

Where was Bethany Hamilton when a tiger shark attacked her?

On her surfboard. The shark took a bite out of the board as she tried to hold on. She lost her left arm. Bethany hasn't given up surfing.

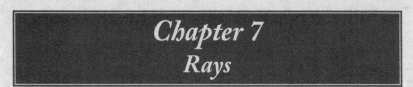

Chapter 7
Rays

What are sharks' closest cousins?

The rays, even though they don't look much alike. Some scientists call them "flat sharks."

How are rays and sharks alike?

Both have skeletons made of rubbery cartilage. And rays, like sharks, would sink if they stopped swimming. Neither have gas-filled swim bladders like bony fish.

RAYS LIKE TO STAY ON THE OCEAN FLOOR.

SHARKS SWIM NEAR THE WATER'S SURFACE.

What's the biggest difference between them?

The ray's huge pectoral fins. These sweep along each side of the ray's head and down the body. They beat up and down so rays seem to fly through the water—mostly to escape hungry sharks!

FASTER!!! HE'S GAINING ON US!

How many different kinds of rays are there?

About 500 species. Rays are found in all oceans. There are even some river rays that live in freshwater.

Where do stingrays get their name?

From the one or more spines on the top side of their long tails. These spines, or "stingers," contain sacs of venom.

How big are stingrays?

Most are about two feet long. The largest are six feet wide and fourteen feet long, including the tail. Rays spend most of the day buried in the sand close to beaches.

How do rays find food?

Most feed along the seafloor. That's because their mouths are located under their heads. Some like to eat clams. Eagle rays can squeeze their pectoral fins together to pop the clams out of the mud. Bands of flat, crushing teeth in the ray's mouth crack open the shellfish. Then the juicy pieces are swallowed.

TRUTH or MYTH?

Stingrays are **aggressive** animals, shooting their poisonous spines.

MYTH! The animal isn't able to shoot its venom. The spine must come in contact with the victim's skin to cause damage.

Can people swim with stingrays?

Some do. There's a place in Grand Cayman in the Caribbean Sea called "Stingray City." Visitors can swim among these animals and feed them by hand.

How was Steve Irwin, the Australian conservationist and TV's "Crocodile Hunter," killed in 2006?

By a stingray. It was an accident. A stingray whipped its tail with the poisonous barb into Steve's chest, hitting his heart. He died within minutes.

Do rays produce electric shocks?

Some do. The electricity comes from large muscles on the side of their bodies, like linked batteries. When threatened, electric rays can release up to 220 volts. That's enough power to turn on a light bulb. Be careful if you step on one. You'll feel the shock.

What's the biggest species of ray?

The manta ray, reaching 3,000 pounds. That's as big as a cow. Some are huge, with a wing span of 20 feet across.

How does it breathe?

The manta ray has gill slits on its underbelly. These take in oxygen from the water.

TRUTH or MYTH?

Mantas are monster-sized, but they aren't dangerous predators.

TRUTH! They're harmless filter feeders. Mantas use their tiny teeth to take plankton from the water. The two large lobes on their heads guide a steady stream of plankton into their wide mouths. Mantas often swim together to feed in shallow water.

When are manta rays a threat to people?

Manta rays are known to take high leaps out of the water. They only threaten people if one of them happens to land on a person.

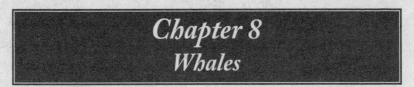

What did whales look like about 49 million years ago?

Some looked a lot like crocodiles. The name of one prehistoric whale, *Ambulocctus*, means "walking whale." It may have fed on animals that came to the water's edge to drink.

What happened next in the fossil record?

These four-legged whales joined other sea monsters and moved into the ocean to live permanently. Over time, they exchanged their limbs for fins. Today, there are two whale groups: the *toothed* whales, which include dolphins, porpoises, orcas, and the huge sperm whale; and the second group, the *toothless* **baleen** whales.

TRUTH or MYTH?

Orcas are known as killer whales.

TRUTH! Orcas are a type of dolphin. They're big and can reach
thirty feet in length.

How did orcas get a bad nickname?

Years ago, Spanish whalers called them "whale killers"
because they hunted whales. By mistake, "whale killers" got
mistranslated to "killer whales," and the legend began.

How do orcas locate their prey?

They use a process called **echolocation**. Whales emit sounds that echo back to help them locate the animals they're hunting.

TRUTH or MYTH?

Orcas like to travel alone, like great white sharks.

MYTH! They're social animals. They travel in family groups called **pods** of four to forty killer whales. Pod members cooperate to capture and kill prey.

ORCAS HAVE SHARP-TEETHED JAWS.

THEY ARE MEAT EATERS.

How much do orcas eat?

An adult male can eat up to 550 pounds of food per day. They spend a lot of their time hunting and feeding on marine animals.

What are their favorite foods?

Sea lion pups playing on the shore. The killer whale swims close to the beach and grabs the pup in its jaws. Then it flips back into the water and heads out to sea.

Are orcas a threat to humans?

There's no documented evidence of a wild orca killing a human. But there have been times when orcas injured their trainers during live marine shows, usually by accident.

Is the blue whale the world's biggest fish?

It's not a fish, but it is the world's biggest animal. The blue whale is a mammal that breathes air. It doesn't have gills. It needs to swim to the surface to get oxygen.

How big can they get?

Some blue whales reach 100 feet, the length of three school buses. They can weigh up to 150 tons, about the same as twenty-five elephants.

How big are blue whale babies?

These mammals give birth to live young, weighing in around 6,000 pounds. Baby blue whales gain nine pounds every hour on their mom's rich milk.

How does the blue whale get rid of old air?

By blowing out air from the two blowholes on the top of its head. Sometimes the air it breathes out rises 30 feet.

Why hold your nose around a blue whale?

The air from the blowhole smells like rotten fish.

How do blue whales eat?

Not with teeth. They don't have any. Blue whales eat krill, or tiny pink shrimp. They use their baleen-lined jaws to filter the krill from the water as it passes through their mouth.

A BLUE WHALE CAN EAT 40 MILLION KRILL EACH DAY.

THE BIGGEST ANIMAL ON EARTH EATS THE SMALLEST ANIMALS IN THE OCEAN!

TRUTH or MYTH?

The blue whale is the world's loudest animal.

TRUTH! It makes great moaning sounds that rumble across the ocean for hundreds of miles.

Can people hear whale sounds?

Not unless they have special equipment. The sounds are too low-pitched for human ears to pick up. They are meant for other whales to hear.

Why do some giant whales leap out of the water and crash back down?

Scientists aren't sure. It might be a way to communicate with other whales. Or the whale might be trying to knock off whale lice living on its skin.

What is this leaping action called?

Breaching. Humpback whales like to leap. Because of their giant bodies, they make a big splash as they breach and hit the water on their way down.

Chapter 9
Crocodiles

What's the biggest type of crocodile?

The saltwater crocodile. It grows as long as 21 feet and weighs as much as 2,400 pounds. It can eat animals as big as a full-grown water buffalo.

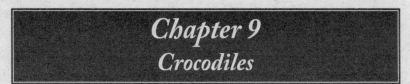

TRUTH or MYTH?

All crocodiles are man-eaters.

MYTH! Only two species are: the Nile crocodile and the Indo-Pacific crocodile. Crocodiles and alligators kill about 2,000 people each year.

Do crocodiles leave the water to hunt prey?

Crocodiles rarely attack on land. But if you're fishing close to the water, stay back at least ten feet. Crocodiles are quick and can grab you fast if you are within reach!

Why are their nostrils set high on their skulls?

So crocodiles can breathe while hiding in the water.

TRUTH or MYTH?

Crocodiles catch prey with their jaws and then chew them.

MYTH! Their jaws are designed for grabbing, not for chewing. When the prey is caught, crocodiles spin the animal in their jaws until it breaks apart.

Why do crocodiles swallow stones?

The stones help grind up the large chunks of food in their stomachs.

What's the biggest crocodile ever caught?

In 2012, a saltwater crocodile was caught in the Philippines. Villagers named it LoLong. This giant measured 20.24 feet and weighed 2,370 pounds.

Some differences between an alligator and a crocodile are:

a) crocs are more aggressive

b) alligators are smaller

c) crocs don't lay eggs, alligators do

d) alligators' snouts are blunt; crocs have pointed snouts

The answers are *a*, *b* and *d*. Both lay eggs.

What's the main difference between alligators and crocodiles?

The large fourth tooth on the lower jaw. In alligators, this tooth doesn't show when the mouth is closed. In crocodiles, you can see the tooth.

Where do alligators live in the U.S.?

Mostly in Florida and other parts of the southeastern U.S. They are often hunted for their skins.

> IN 1888, JUST TEN HUNTERS KILLED 5,000 ALLIGATORS.

> IN 1907, ONE COMPANY MADE LEATHER OUT OF 500,000 SKINS.

Are alligators better protected today?

The American alligator was in danger of disappearing in 1960. Today, hunting alligators is limited by law.

Chapter 10
Octopuses

Have octopuses been around a long time?

Yes. Ancestors of today's octopus were around 95 million years ago. Some ancient seamen say the legendary Kraken was a giant octopus, not a monster squid.

Why are octopuses called "eight-arm beasts"?

Some grow up to 30 feet across and are strong, even the smaller ones. Try grabbing something from a five-foot octopus holding on with all eight arms! It would take a quarter of a ton of force to get the thing away from the octopus.

TRUTH or MYTH?

The octopus has eight arms, like its cousin the squid.
TRUTH! But the squid also has two tentacles. Octopuses have none.

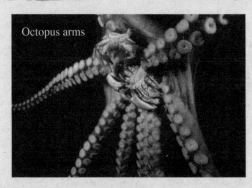

Octopus arms

Where does the octopus get its strength?

From disklike **suckers** on its arms. These act like rubber suction cups. There are as many as 280 per arm, for a total force of 2,240 suction cups.

How do they move?

Octopuses use a built-in siphon to shoot out jets of water. This action propels its body forward.

Where do octopuses lay their eggs?

In their homes under rocks or in cracks on the seabed.

How many eggs can one octopus lay?

A lot. The giant Pacific octopus produces 20,000 to 100,000 eggs. New babies are about the size of a pea, but few survive.

How smart is the giant octopus?

Smart enough to solve complex problems. Scientists have taught these smart animals to solve a maze by trial and error.

How big can an octopus get?

No one knows, but pieces of giant octopuses have been found. One piece, found on the beach in St. Augustine, Florida, in 1876, weighed a few tons. Its arms could have been 75 feet long and 36 inches thick.

Has anyone ever seen one this big?

Navy coxswain John C. Martin on board the USS *Chicopee* in 1941 claimed to have sighted a huge pile of brown seaweed on the water surface. He saw the arms of the beast, looped like a "coil of rope." The "rope" he estimated was 36 inches thick.

How do octopuses act like underwater spies?

They hide in the sandy ocean floor. They keep watch by raising a single eye. They search for food, such as crabs and lobsters, and keep an eye out for predators, like sharks.

How do they protect themselves?

By turning different colors. Their skin has special color cells. The octopus is able to turn its skin the same color as its surroundings. It **camouflages** itself, becoming almost invisible on the seabed.

What trick do they use to escape predators?

They spurt out a cloud of black or purple ink. The ink confuses the attacker while the octopus gets away.

Octopuses attack people.

MYTH! Rarely. Most species are shy and timid. They usually hide in undersea caves or in holes in the sand. They're **nocturnal** animals, exploring mostly at night.

Are they poisonous?

Many have venomous bites. The six-inch blue-ringed octopus, found in Australian waters, has powerful venom. Its bite could kill a person in a matter of minutes.

THE BODY IS THE SIZE OF A GOLF BALL.

ITS BITE CAN CUT THROUGH A DIVER'S WET SUIT.

ITS PARROT-LIKE BEAK DOES THE DAMAGE!

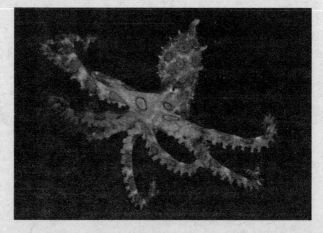

When does the blue-ringed octopus turn blue?

When it's ready to attack, its rings turn bright blue. It's a warning to others of its poisonous bite.

WHY IS IT TURNING BRIGHT BLUE?

TIME TO GET OUT OF HERE!!

Why does the blue-ringed octopus spit on its prey?

To release its deadly **saliva** into the water. Then, the octopus waits for the poison to work. Sometimes the octopus catches, bites, and injects prey directly.

Chapter 11
Stinging Jellyfish

What are adult jellyfish called?

Medusas. They have an umbrella-shaped body, or bell, and swinging tentacles.

How big are they?

There are about 200 different species of true jellyfish. The Nomura jellyfish, found along the coasts of China and Japan, can weigh up to 450 pounds.

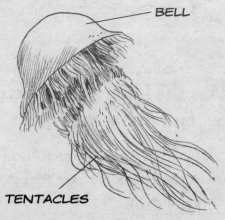

BELL

TENTACLES

66

How fast do they grow?

In six months, the Nomura jellyfish grows from the size of a grain of rice to the size of a small car.

Are they dangerous?

To a passing fish, but not to a human. The poison from a sting quickly wears off.

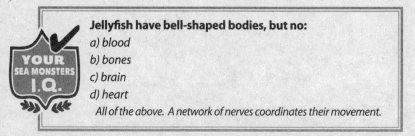

Jellyfish have bell-shaped bodies, but no:

a) blood
b) bones
c) brain
d) heart

All of the above. A network of nerves coordinates their movement.

Is the Portuguese man-of-war a true jellyfish?

No, it's actually a *siphonophore*—a colony of animals, not an individual. It stings, but that sting isn't fatal.

ENGLISH SAILORS NAMED IT AFTER A PORTUGUESE FIGHTING SHIP.

THE SHIP'S SAIL LOOKED LIKE THE FLOATING JELLYFISH.

How big is it?

The Portuguese man-of-war can have tentacles as long as a blue whale. Its stings are so painful that humans often faint from the pain.

Can you get rid of a jellyfish by cutting it into pieces?

No. If you do, each piece can grow into a new adult animal.

PLOP! PLOP!

The box jellyfish is the deadliest sea creature of all.
TRUTH! It kills more people than sharks, crocodiles, and stonefish combined each year.

Why is the box jellyfish hard to see?

It's made up of 95 percent water, so it's almost invisible.

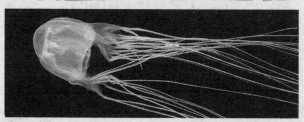

ONE BOX JELLYFISH CAN HAVE 60 TENTACLES.

ONE TENTACLE CAN KILL UP TO 50 HUMANS!

How dangerous is it to swimmers?

Very. People are easily stung by box jellyfish. The pain is terrible. One sting can cause death in three minutes!

BEACH CLOSED!
BEWARE OF BOX JELLYFISH

Chapter 12
Piranhas

What are piranhas?

They're small freshwater fish that live in the rivers of South America.

THE NAME COMES FROM THE TUPI INDIANS.

"PIRAI" MEANS FISH AND "ANHA" MEANS TOOTH.

How big are they?

They range from an inch or two to about two feet in size.

Are they powerful?

Their jaws are. They have a single row of daggerlike teeth on each jaw. With a few bites, the black piranha can chew through a man's wrist.

How good is their sense of smell?

Piranhas can detect a drop of blood in 53 gallons of water.

Are they dangerous?

Not all species are. Many are vegetarian. They eat fruit and berries that fall into the river.

TRUTH or MYTH?

South American piranhas have been known to eat people.

MYTH! They have attacked people, but there is no evidence that they have actually killed people.

What happens to piranhas in the dry season?

They can be stranded in small lakes with little food—and they can be aggressive when hungry. They gang up in a school. Working together, they attack birds, rodents, frogs, and other animals.

IN BRAZIL, PIRANHAS KILL ABOUT 1,200 CATTLE EVERY YEAR.

THE CATTLE COME TO THE WATER'S EDGE TO DRINK.

Do piranhas get along with each other?

Not always. Even though they hunt together, they sometimes use their killer jaws on one another, especially when excited.

Indians of the Amazon use piranha teeth:
a) for sharpening darts
b) as a cutting tool
c) for sewing clothes
d) for shaving
The answers are *a*, *b*, and *d*.

Who snacks on piranhas?

Indians in Paraguay do. The fish is delicious—like trout. People cook them on spits, along with other river fish.

Is it legal to own piranhas as pets in your aquarium?

Not in some states. Sometimes people release these pets into rivers and lakes. One was caught by Florida wildlife officials in 1970. But most U.S. waters are too cold for piranhas to survive.

How long does it take piranhas to pick clean the bones of a dead animal?

Only minutes. A school of piranhas can eat the flesh off a dead monkey in five minutes. A human corpse—a victim of an accident on the river—can be eaten, but not a live person.

How did piranhas get such a bad reputation?

From U.S. president Teddy Roosevelt. He visited Brazil in 1913 on a hunting trip through the Amazon rain forest. To impress him, some fishermen blocked off part of a river and starved the piranhas for a few days. Then they pushed a cow into the water. It was quickly torn apart by the hungry piranhas. Roosevelt later wrote about these vicious creatures in his book *Through the Brazilian Wilderness*. He called them "the most ferocious fish in the world."

Chapter 13
Extreme Sea Animals

What fish has the head of a dragon and the curly tail of a monkey?

The sea horse. It swims upright slowly through the water. It can remain still for long periods, hanging on to sea grass and coral with its tail.

How many kinds of sea horse are there?

About 36 species around the world.

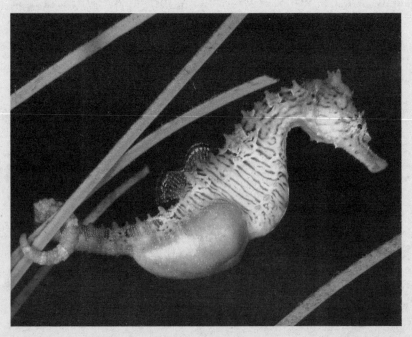

Sea horses hide from predators by
camouflaging themselves.
TRUTH! They can change color in minutes, turning from black or gray to
yellow or orange.

How much do they eat?

They eat all the time. Sea horses use their long snouts to eat 3,000 tiny shrimp every day.

Do male sea horses babysit their young?

They do a lot more than that, at least at the beginning. They're the only animal species in which the male carries the babies before birth. The female places about 200 eggs in a pouch in the male's belly. A month later, baby sea horses emerge from the pouch and swim away.

Where does the world's only sea-going lizard live?

The Galapagos Islands, off the coast of Ecuador, South America. These marine iguanas are strange-looking creatures. They have wrinkled black skin, small heads and eyes, and a pointed ridge down their backs. Marine iguanas crowd together on volcanic rocks on shore when not feeding in the water.

When do the males butt heads?

When fighting over a female. The males do this for up to five hours at a time.

Why do marine iguanas sneeze a lot?

To get rid of too much salt in their bodies. Visitors don't get too close, or they'll be covered with flying liquid!

Are there snakes that live in the sea?

Yes, and some are more poisonous than any on land. Most sea snakes live in the warm waters of the Pacific and Indian Oceans.

TRUTH or MYTH?

Sea snakes can stay underwater for several hours.

TRUTH! Most sea snakes have lungs. They can dive down to about 300 feet, and stay under for hours on one lungful of air. They also take in oxygen from the water through their skin.

How big can sea snakes grow?

Most are about three feet long, but some can reach eight feet. They mostly feed on fish and rarely attack people.

Is "Frankenfish" the name of a real fish?

No. These strange-looking creatures caused quite a sensation when they mysteriously crawled out of a pond in Crofton, Maryland, in 2002.

What did they look like?

Like "snakeheads," as the local people called them. The creatures were able to breathe air and walk short distances on land. They were aggressive, and fed on frogs, birds, and small mammals.

Where did they come from?

A live Asian food market in the area. The Frankenfish were actually a rare species, mostly from Thailand, that were discarded by local restaurants. Six adult snakeheads and more than a hundred juvenile fish were found and destroyed. Several horror movies were made about this "snakehead invasion."

What fish is the fastest?

The sailfish, speeding up to 68 mph.

What's the world's largest freshwater fish?

The Mekong giant catfish, found mostly in Vietnam, holds the Guinness Record. It can grow up to 660 pounds and ten and a half feet in length.

Chapter 14
Creatures of the Deep Sea

Where do the strange-looking anglerfish live?

In sunless waters, thousands of feet below the surface. They have big heads and fierce-looking teeth.

How big are they?

There's a big difference in size between males and females. Males are much smaller, about one-twelfth the size of females.

What's so strange about their eating habits?

The little males have pointed teeth, so they can hold on tight to the larger females. Once attached, they become **parasites**. They live and feed through the female's body.

How does the female anglerfish capture other fish?

She uses the front spine of her dorsal fin. It glows and acts as a fishing rod and lure. The anglerfish wiggles the lure to attract passing fish. They are quickly snapped up by the anglerfish's deadly teeth.

How do some deep-sea animals get around in the dark ocean?

Like the anglerfish, they depend on **bioluminescence**. They have light-producing bacteria present in their living tissue.

IN WORLD WAR II, THE JAPANESE USED BIOLUMINESCENT BACTERIA TO LIGHT THEIR HOMES DURING BOMBING BLACKOUTS.

YOUR SEA MONSTERS I.Q.

What percentage of sharks are bioluminescent?

a) 15%

b) 38%

c) 10%

d) 7%

The answer is *c*. Light cells on their underside cause some sharks to glow like a firefly. It helps hide them by blending in with sunlight filtering down from above.

Is an eel a fish or a snake?

A fish. Eels don't have scales and pelvic fins. They are long and tube-shaped, and glide in the water the way snakes move on land.

Where can you find gulper eels?

In very deep waters. Their bodies are tiny, but their mouths and teeth are huge. Gulper eels stay still in the dark and wait for another fish to swim by. Then they open their mouths wide, like an umbrella, to catch the fish.

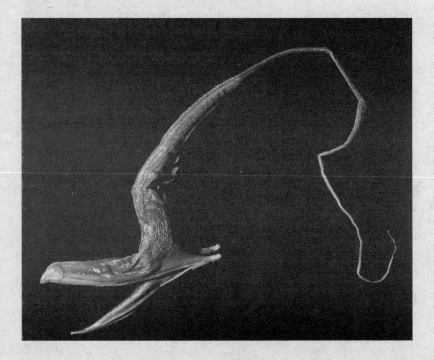

Why is the viperfish so fierce-looking?

Its fang-like teeth give it a terrifying look. But it's small, so it's not a threat to humans.

What's the world's most poisonous fish?

The stonefish. It has 13 spines filled with venom on its back. One sting can lead to death in a few hours if not treated.

Why is the stonefish so dangerous?

It has great camouflage ability. It lies hidden until ready to release its deadly poison.

TRUTH or MYTH?

The cookie-cutter shark regularly takes bites out of blue whales.

TRUTH! The bite leaves a scar the shape of a cookie on the whales' skin.

Do you want to be kissed by the cookie-cutter shark?

Only if you want to lose a chunk of your flesh! This small shark has suction-cup lips that hold on to its victim. The shark twists itself around, while its razor-sharp lower teeth bite out a cookie-shaped piece of flesh.

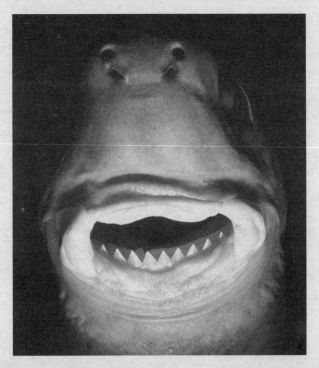

Where does the blobfish live?

Off the Australian coast, from 2,000 to 3,900 feet below the water's surface.

Why is the blobfish called
the world's ugliest fish?

The flesh of the blobfish is a jellylike mass. It has no muscles. When taken out of its deepwater home, it just loses shape. It looks like a "blob."

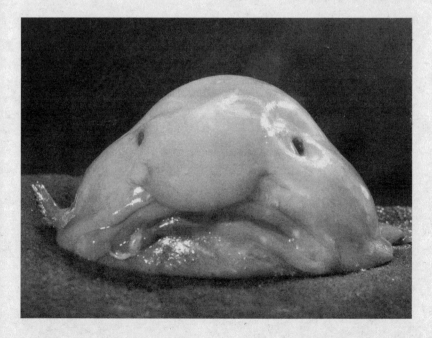

Chapter 15
Deep-Sea Explorers

Who was the first person to dive deep into the sea?

Dr. Will Beebe, in 1934. He dived over 3,000 feet in a **submersible** he called the Bathysphere. It was designed by the American engineer Otis Barton for studying deep-sea animals in their natural habitat.

TRUTH or MYTH?

Beebe and Barton took a lot of photographs.

MYTH! There weren't any good underwater cameras at the time. But Beebe took notes of what he saw from the Bathysphere's three windows. Later, illustrations were made of what he observed.

Who is credited with the invention of modern scuba diving?

Jacques Cousteau, the famous French underwater ocean explorer. He used the first Aqua-Lung scuba technology when filming a movie underwater in 1943.

What was his famous research ship?

The *Calypso*. It became Cousteau's traveling laboratory and base for diving and filming his underwater expeditions.

How did Cousteau introduce ocean life to people around the world?

He created *The Undersea World of Jacques Cousteau* and *The Cousteau Odyssey* series for American TV. In all, he wrote more than 50 books and made 120 TV documentaries. Many featured his "yellow submarine" submersible launched from the *Calypso*.

CALYPSO

Who is one of today's best-known underwater archaeologists?

Dr. Robert Ballard, a former Navy officer and professor working out of the University of Rhode Island's Graduate School of Oceanography.

How did Ballard get interested in sea exploration?

He grew up by the sea in California. When he was a kid, he read Jules Verne's novel *20,000 Leagues Under the Sea* and was hooked!

What famous shipwrecks did Ballard investigate?

a) RMS *Titanic*

b) the battleship *Bismarck*

c) the aircraft carrier USS *Yorktown*

d) RMS *Lusitania*

All of the above. In 2002, Ballard found the wreck of President John F. Kennedy's PT-109. The boat was sunk by the Japanese off the Solomon Islands during World War II.

Who made the deepest solo dive ever?

The marine biologist and undersea explorer Sylvia Earle. She reached 1,250 feet below the surface. Earle wore a special suit to control water pressure and temperature.

Glossary

abyss—a hole so deep that it cannot be measured

aggressive—ready and willing to fight

baleen—bristles inside the mouths of some whales to catch krill

bioluminescence—the ability of some living plants and animals to produce light

breach—the leap of a whale above the surface of the water

camouflage—able to hide itself and blend in with its surroundings

carnivore—a meat eater

cartilage—a very strong but bendable material found in some parts of the body

current—a strong movement of water in one direction

echolocation—the use of sound waves and echoes to detect the distant location of objects in water or space

extinct—no longer existing

flexible—capable of bending

folk tradition—customs, beliefs, and stories that are passed down from one generation to the next

food chain—a series of related organisms, each one feeding upon a smaller one in the group

fossil—remains from a plant or animal that lived long ago and that you can see in some rocks

fossil record—the remains of a plant or animal that has been preserved as evidence of what happened long ago

gill—the body part that a fish uses for breathing

glacier—a very large area of ice that moves slowly over a wide area of land

habitat—a place where a plant or animal naturally lives or grows

hoax—an act that is meant to trick people

invertebrate—a type of animal with no backbone

krill—very small ocean creatures that are the main food of some whales

lateral line—a body organ in fish that detects movements in the water

metabolism—the chemical process by which an animal uses food and water to grow and to make energy

migration—movement from one region or place to another

nocturnal—active mainly during the night

Pangaea—the name of the large landmass on Earth that existed 250 million years ago before it broke apart to form the seven continents

parasite—an animal or plant that lives on another animal or plant and gets its food from it

plankton—tiny animal and plant life that drifts in large numbers in an ocean or lake

pod—a small group of ocean animals, usually dolphins or whales

predator—an animal that lives by killing and eating other animals

prehistoric—existing in the time before people could write

prey—an animal that is hunted and eaten by another animal for food

saliva—the liquid in the mouth that makes it easier to swallow food

sedimentary—a kind of rock formed by deposits of organic matter or minerals

submersible—a vehicle able to be used underwater

sucker—a part of an animal's body that can attach to things

tsunami—a high, large ocean wave that is produced by an undersea earthquake

venom—a poison produced by an animal

vertebrate—an animal that has a backbone

If you like *History Busters:*
The Truth (and Myths) about Sea Monsters,
you'll love discovering the facts (and myths) in

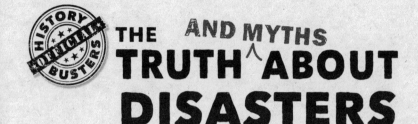

HISTORY OFFICIAL BUSTERS

THE **AND MYTHS**
TRUTH ^ ABOUT
DISASTERS

HISTORY OFFICIAL BUSTERS

THE **AND MYTHS**
TRUTH ^ ABOUT
THE PRESIDENTS

HISTORY OFFICIAL BUSTERS

THE **AND MYTHS**
TRUTH ^ ABOUT
THANKSGIVING